W9-CKI-358

BULLET TRAINS

BY DENNY VON FINN

TORQUE ™

BELLWETHER MEDIA • MINNEAPOLIS, MN

Are you ready to take it to the extreme?
Torque books thrust you into the action-packed world
of sports, vehicles, and adventure. These books may
include dirt, smoke, fire, and dangerous stunts.
WARNING: read at your own risk.

This edition first published in 2010 by Bellwether Media, Inc.

No part of this publication may be reproduced in whole or in part without written permission of the publisher. For information regarding permission, write to Bellwether Media, Inc., Attention: Permissions Department, 5357 Penn Avenue South, Minneapolis, MN, 55419.

Library of Congress Cataloging-in-Publication Data

Von Finn, Denny.
  Bullet trains / by Denny Von Finn.
     p. cm. – (Torque : the world's fastest)
  Includes bibliographical references and index.
  Summary: "Amazing photography accompanies engaging information about bullet trains.
The combination of high-interest subject matter and light text is intended for students in grades 3 through 7"
–Provided by publisher.
  ISBN 978-1-60014-286-4 (hardcover : alk. paper)
  1. High speed trains–Juvenile literature. I. Title.

 TF148.V65 2010
 385'.22--dc22

                              2009013255

Printed in the United States of America.

CONTENTS

What Are Bullet Trains?

Bullet trains are high-speed trains. They travel more than 124 miles (200 kilometers) per hour. They are smooth and **streamlined**. The name "bullet train" comes from their speed and shape. Today, bullet trains are popular forms of **intercity** travel in Europe and Asia.

Bullet trains got their start in Japan. This small country's population grew rapidly in the 1950s. Japan's trains and roads became crowded. People needed a new way to get around.

Japanese officials hoped a new kind of train would solve their transportation problems. The government opened the first **Shinkansen** in 1964. It ran 320 miles (515 kilometers) between the cities of Tokyo and Osaka. These first Shinkansen trains reached 135 miles (217 kilometers) per hour!

France's **TGV** became the world's second high-speed passenger rail line in 1981. In 2007, a TGV train set the world speed record for a wheeled train. It reached a speed of 357.2 miles (574.8 kilometers) per hour on a **trial run**.

Bullet Train Technology

Most high-speed trains are pulled by electric **locomotives**. A locomotive is the motorized vehicle that pulls or pushes a train. A bullet train's locomotive gets power from wires above the train. These wires are called **catenaries**. Some TGV locomotives can create 12,000 **horsepower**. That's the same amount of power created by 60 normal cars!

Fast Fact

Electric locomotives create less air pollution than locomotives powered by diesel fuel. This makes them desirable in areas with many people.

High-speed trains need special **infrastructure**. Tracks have long, gentle curves. This helps decrease the effects of **centrifugal force** felt by passengers. Some high-speed trains are designed to tilt as they travel around curves. This also lessens centrifugal force.

Bullet trains ride on very long **rails**. The rail connections need to be smooth. This allows the train to travel fast.

Many high-speed **rights-of-way** are surrounded by fences. This keeps animals and people off the tracks. Rights-of-way also avoid **grade crossings**. Cars can't cross over the tracks and force trains to stop.

The Future of Bullet Trains

Bullet trains have an exciting future. The most important bullet train development is maglev. Maglev is short for "magnetic levitation." Magnetic forces inside the train and on the ground suspend the train above the track. They also move it forward. There are no wheels and no **friction** between the train and the track.

The only maglev passenger train in operation is in Shanghai, China. It travels 267 miles (430 kilometers) per hour. In 2003, an experimental maglev train in Japan reached 361 miles (581 kilometers) per hour!

In 2008, California voters approved a high-speed rail line. It will connect Los Angeles and San Francisco. These trains could have a top speed of 220 miles (354 kilometers) per hour. They would rival bullet trains anywhere in the world!

Bullet trains are being built all over the world. New technology will help them reach faster speeds. Korea hopes its KTX bullet train will regularly travel at nearly 250 miles (402 kilometers) per hour.

Bullet trains will also be much more efficient. This means they will make less noise and use less energy. Bullet trains are a safe, cheap, and fast way to travel!

Fast Fact

There are plans to create high-speed rail systems in India, Argentina, South Africa, and Russia.

GLOSSARY

catenaries—overhead wires that provide electricity to power locomotives

centrifugal force—the force that pulls at an object as it travels around a bend

friction—resistance created when two objects rub together

grade crossings—points where train tracks and roadways cross each other

horsepower—a unit used to measure the power created by an engine

infrastructure—objects such as tracks and stations that trains require to operate

intercity—a train service that travels between two or more cities

locomotive—the motorized vehicle that pulls a train

rails—the long pieces of steel on which a train rides

rights-of-way—the paths that train tracks follow; many are surrounded by fences so animals and people cannot get onto high-speed train tracks.

Shinkansen—a Japanese word that means "new rail lines" and describes the country's high-speed train lines

streamlined—designed to easily move through the air

TGV—France's high-speed rail system; an abbreviation of *train á grande vitesse*, the French term for "high-speed train."

trial run—a test of a new train that is made with no passengers on board

AT THE LIBRARY

Cefrey, Holly. *High Speed Trains*. New York, N.Y.: Rosen, 2001.

Dubowski, Mark. *Superfast Trains*. New York, N.Y.: Bearport, 2006.

Hofer, Charles. *Bullet Trains*. New York, N.Y.: PowerKids Press, 2008.

ON THE WEB

Learning more about bullet trains is as easy as 1, 2, 3.

1. Go to www.factsurfer.com.

2. Enter "bullet trains" into the search box.

3. Click the "Surf" button and you will see a list of related Web sites.

With factsurfer.com, finding more information is just a click away.

The images in this book are reproduced through the courtesy of: Holger Mette, front cover; Shiyali, pp. 4-5; Brian Lovell / Age Fotostock, pp. 6-7; Topic Photo Agency / Age Fotostock, pp. 8-9; DAJ / Getty Images, p. 10; Bernd Mellmann / Alamy, pp. 11, 16-17; China Photos / Stringer / Getty Images, pp. 12-13; JUNG YEON-JE / Stringer / Getty Images, p. 14; Jupiterimages / Getty Images, p. 15; Kevin Foy / Alamy, pp. 18-19; LEE JIN-MAN / Associated Press, p. 20; Peter Horree / Alamy, p. 21

Mercury

by Derek Zobel

Consultant:
Duane Quam, M.S. Physics
Chair, Minnesota State
Academic Science Standards
Writing Committee

BLASTOFF! READERS
3

BELLWETHER MEDIA · MINNEAPOLIS, MN

Note to Librarians, Teachers, and Parents:

Blastoff! Readers are carefully developed by literacy experts and combine standards-based content with developmentally appropriate text.

Level 1 provides the most support through repetition of high-frequency words, light text, predictable sentence patterns, and strong visual support.

Level 2 offers early readers a bit more challenge through varied simple sentences, increased text load, and less repetition of high-frequency words.

Level 3 advances early-fluent readers toward fluency through increased text and concept load, less reliance on visuals, longer sentences, and more literary language.

Level 4 builds reading stamina by providing more text per page, increased use of punctuation, greater variation in sentence patterns, and increasingly challenging vocabulary.

Level 5 encourages children to move from "learning to read" to "reading to learn" by providing even more text, varied writing styles, and less familiar topics.

Whichever book is right for your reader, Blastoff! Readers are the perfect books to build confidence and encourage a love of reading that will last a lifetime!

This edition first published in 2010 by Bellwether Media, Inc.

No part of this publication may be reproduced in whole or in part without written permission of the publisher. For information regarding permission, write to Bellwether Media, Inc., Attention: Permissions Department, 5357 Penn Avenue South, Minneapolis, MN 55419.

Library of Congress Cataloging-in-Publication Data

Zobel, Derek, 1983-
Mercury / by Derek Zobel.
    p. cm. – (Blastoff! readers. Exploring space)
Includes bibliographical references and index.
Summary: "Introductory text and full-color images explore the physical characteristics and discovery of the planet Mercury. Intended for students in kindergarten through third grade"–Provided by publisher.
ISBN 978-1-60014-402-8 (hardcover : alk. paper)
1. Mercury (Planet)–Juvenile literature. I. Title.
QB611.Z63 2010
523.41–dc22   2009038273

Text copyright © 2010 by Bellwether Media, Inc.
Printed in the United States of America, North Mankato, MN.

010110   1149

Contents

Mercury is a **planet** named after the **Roman god** of speed. It is the smallest planet in the **solar system**.

Mercury is 3,032 miles
(4,879 kilometers) across.
Earth is almost three times
as wide.

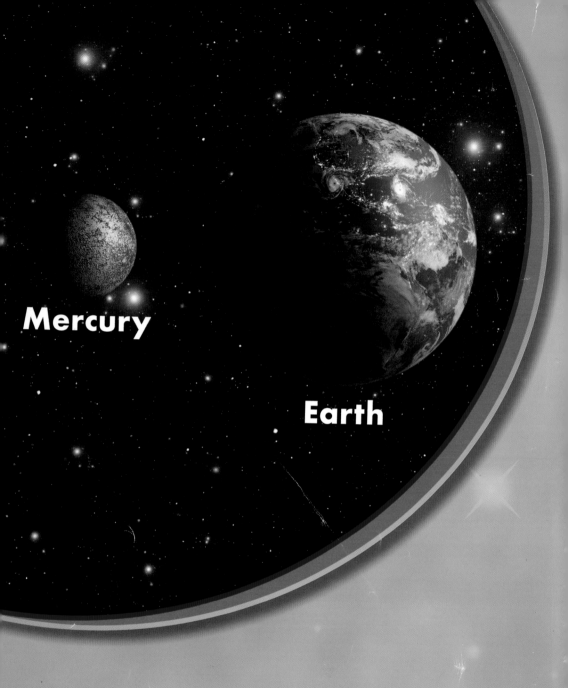

Mercury

Earth

Mercury is much smaller than Earth.
It could fit inside Earth 18 times.

Jupiter is the biggest planet in the solar system. Mercury could fit inside Jupiter 24,462 times!

Mercury

Jupiter

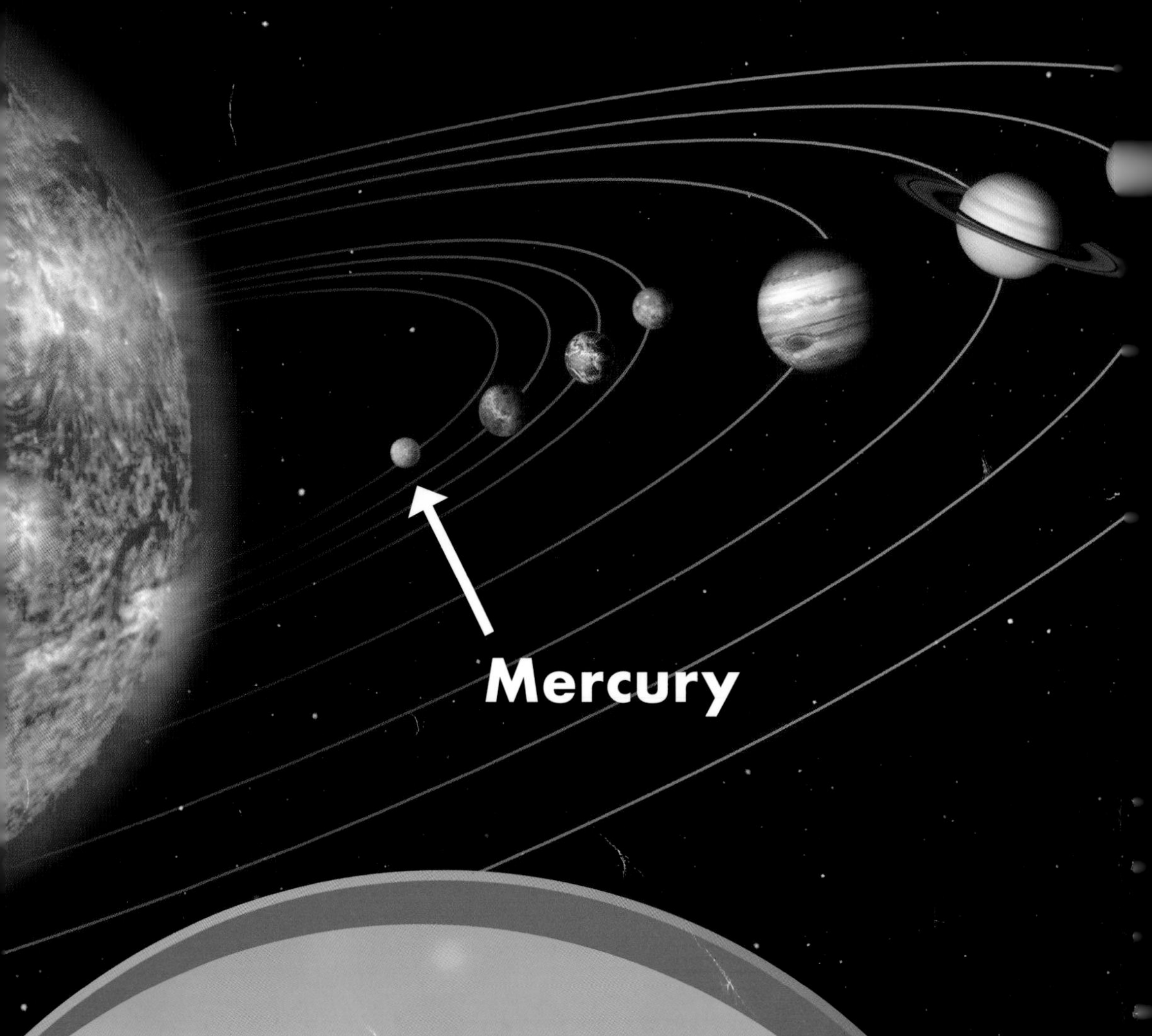

Mercury

All of the planets in the
solar system **orbit** the sun.
Mercury is the planet closest
to the sun.

8

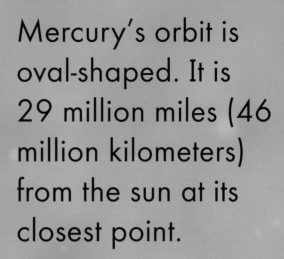

Mercury's orbit is oval-shaped. It is 29 million miles (46 million kilometers) from the sun at its closest point.

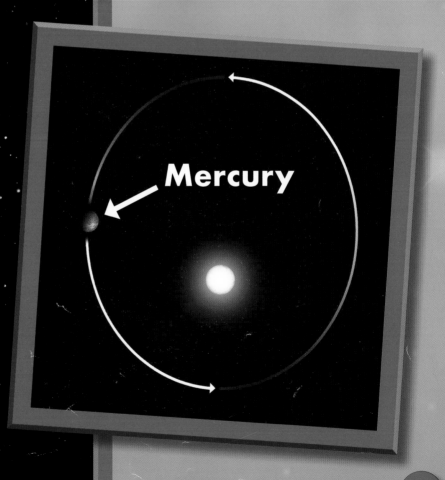

Mercury

A day is the amount of time it takes a planet to spin once on its **axis**.

axis

Mercury spins very slowly. A day on Mercury equals 59 Earth days!

A year is the time it takes a planet to go around the sun once. It takes Earth 365 days to go around the sun.

Earth

Mercury

Mercury goes around the sun faster than any other planet. Mercury orbits the sun in just 88 Earth days.

840°F (450°C) ⟶

Mercury has very high and very low temperatures. Temperatures can reach 840° Fahrenheit (450° Celsius).

-275°F (-170°C)

The temperature can drop to
-275°F (-170°C) at night.

Mercury's surface is similar to
the surface of Earth's moon.
It has flat plains and
steep cliffs.

These features formed when lava from **volcanoes** flowed over the surface.

Mercury also has many **craters**.
Craters form when **meteorites**
crash into Mercury's surface.

The largest crater is the Caloris Basin. It is 800 miles (1,300 kilometers) across.

Messenger

Messenger is a **space probe** that was launched in 2004. Its mission is to explore Mercury's surface and environment.

Scientists will continue sending probes to Mercury. We still have a lot to learn about the solar system's smallest planet!

Glossary

axis—an imaginary line that runs through the center of a planet; a planet spins on its axis.

craters—holes made when meteorites or other space objects crash into moons, planets, or other space objects

meteorites—chunks of rock or other matter that have fallen from space

orbit—to travel around the sun or other object in space

planet—a large, round space object that orbits the sun and is alone in its orbit

Roman god—a god worshipped by the people of ancient Rome; Mercury is the Roman god of speed.

solar system—the sun and all the objects that orbit it; the solar system has planets, moons, comets, and asteroids.

space probe—a spacecraft that explores planets and other space objects and sends information back to Earth; space probes do not carry people.

volcanoes—holes in a planet's surface through which melted rock called lava flows; over time the lava can form a mountain.

To Learn More

AT THE LIBRARY
Kerrod, Robin. *Mercury and Venus*. Minneapolis, Minn.: Lerner Publications, 2000.

Loewen, Nancy. *Nearest to the Sun: The Planet Mercury*. Minneapolis, Minn.: Picture Window Books, 2008.

Taylor-Butler, Christine. *Mercury*. New York, N.Y.: Children's Press, 2008.

ON THE WEB
Learning more about Mercury is as easy as 1, 2, 3.

1. Go to www.factsurfer.com.

2. Enter "Mercury" into the search box.

3. Click the "Surf" button and you will see a list of related Web sites.

With factsurfer.com, finding more information is just a click away.

BLASTOFF! JIMMY CHALLENGE
Blastoff! Jimmy is hidden somewhere in this book. Can you find him? If you need help, you can find a hint at the bottom of page 24.

Index

Blastoff! Jimmy Challenge (from page 23).
Hint: Go to page 11 and gaze at the stars.